IN THE KIBBLE PALACE

D0795305

IN THE KIBBLE
P·A·L·A·C·E

NEW & SELECTED POEMS

Stewart Conn

BLOODAXE BOOKS

Copyright © Stewart Conn 1967, 1968, 1972, 1978, 1987

ISBN: 1 85224 033 4

First published 1987 by
Bloodaxe Books Ltd,
P.O. Box 1SN,
Newcastle upon Tyne NE99 1SN.

Bloodaxe Books Ltd acknowledges
the financial assistance of Northern Arts.

LEGAL NOTICE
All rights reserved. No part of this book may be
reproduced, stored in a retrieval system, or
transmitted in any form, or by any means, electronic,
mechanical, photocopying, recording or otherwise,
without the prior permission of the publisher.

Typesetting by Bryan Williamson, Manchester.

Printed in Great Britain by
Bell & Bain Limited, Glasgow, Scotland.

For Judy, Arthur and Ian

Acknowledgements

The poems in Sections I and II are from *Thunder in the Air* (Akros Publications, 1967), *The Chinese Tower* (Macdonald, 1967), *Stoats in the Sunlight* (Hutchinson, 1968), *An Ear to the Ground* (Hutchinson, 1972) and *Under the Ice* (Hutchinson, 1978); and from *Modern Poets in Focus 3* (Corgi Books, 1971) and *A Sense of Belonging* (Blackie, 1977). 'Marriage a Mountain Ridge' first appeared in *Poetry* (Chicago).

For the poems in Section III acknowledgements are due to *Akros, Aquarius, Cencrastus, Chapman, Encounter, Helix, Lines, The Listener, London Magazine, New Edinburgh Review, New Statesman, PN Review, Poetry Review, The Scotsman, Scottish Review, Verse, Words* and to the BBC and Radio Clyde. Also to the editors of *12 More Modern Scottish Poets* (Hodder & Stoughton, 1986), *Edinburgh and the Borders in Verse* (Secker & Warburg, 1983), *Speak to the Hills* (Aberdeen University Press, 1985), *Natural Light* (Paul Harris/Waterfront, 1985), *New Poetry 8* (Hutchinson/Arts Council – P.E.N., 1982), and *Antologia Nowej Poezji Brytyjskiej* (Czytelnik, Warsaw, 1983).

Contents

III.   NEW POEMS

I.

Todd

My father's white uncle became
   Arthritic and testamental in
   Lyrical stages. He held cardinal sin
Was misuse of horses, then any game

Won on the sabbath. A Clydesdale
   To him was not bells and sugar or declension
   From paddock, but primal extension
Of rock and soil. Thundered nail

Turned to sacred bolt. And each night
   In the stable he would slaver and slave
   At cracked hooves, or else save
Bowls of porridge for just the right

Beast. I remember I lied
   To him once, about oats: then I felt
   The brand of his loving tongue, the belt
Of his own horsey breath. But he died,

When the mechanised tractor came to pass.
   Now I think of him neighing to some saint
   In a simple heaven or, beyond complaint,
Leaning across a fence and munching grass.

'Harelaw'

Ploughlands roll where limekilns lay
   Seeping in craters. Where once dense
   Fibres oozed against gatepost and fence
Till staples burst, firm wheatfields sway;
   And where quarries reeked, intense

With honeysuckle, a truck dumps load
   Upon load of earth, of ash and slag
   For the raking. Spliced hawsers drag
Roots out and wrench the rabbit wood
   Apart as though some cuckoo fugue

Had rioted. On this mossy slope
   That raindrops used to drill and drum
   Through dusk, no nightjar flits nor numb
Hawk hangs as listening foxes lope
   And prowl; no lilac shadows thumb

The heavy air. This holt was mine
   To siege and plunder; here I caged
   Rare beasts or swayed royally on the agèd
Backs of horses – here hacked my secret sign,
   Strode, wallowed, ferreted, rampaged.

But acres crumple and the farm's new image
   Spreads over the old. As I face
   Its change, a truck tips litter; hens assess
Bright tins, then peck and squawk their rage.
   The truck spurts flame and I have no redress.

Ayrshire Farm

Every new year's morning the farmers
Would meet at 'Harelaw' with their guns
For the shoot. Mungo red in the face,
Matthew hale as a tree, John huge
In old leather. The others in dribs
And drabs, shotguns over their shoulders,
Bags flopping at their sides, collars up.

We'd set out across the north park,
The glaur on our leggings freezing
As we left the shelter of the knowes.
No dogs. Even the ferrets on this day
Of days were left squealing behind
Their wire. We'd fan out, taking
The slope at a steady tramp.

Mungo always aimed first, blasting away
At nothing. Hugh cursed under his breath;
The rest of us kept going. Suddenly
The hares would rise from the bracken-clumps
And go looping downhill. I remember
The banks alive with scuts, the dead
Gorse-tufts splattered with shot.

One by one the haversacks filled,
The blood dripping from them, staining
The snow. Matthew still in front,
Directing the others; the sun red
Behind its dyke, the wind rising.
And myself bringing up the rear,
Pretending I was lost, become the quarry.

Three blasts on a whistle, the second
Time round. And, in from the sleet,
We would settle on bales with bottles
And flasks, to divide the spoils. The bodies
Slit, and hung on hooks to drip. The rest
Thrown smoking on the midden. The dogs
Scrabbling on their chains, Todd's stallion

Rearing at the reek of blood. Then in
To the fire and a roaring new year:
Old Martha and Mima scuffling to and fro,
Our men's bellies filling, hands
Slowly thawing. And for me, off to bed,
A pig in the sheets, the oil lamp
Throwing shadows of rabbits on the wall.

*

Last winter I covered the same ground
On my own, no gun. Martha and Mima
Have gone to rest. Todd has tethered
His horses under the hill. Mungo, too,
From a fall at the baling. Yet my breathing
Seemed to make their shapes; and Matthew's
And Hugh's, and my own bringing up the rear.

At the road-end I stopped and stood
For some time, just listening. My hands
Growing numb. Then I crossed the track
To where a single rabbit lay twitching,
Big-headed, eyes bulging, in pain.
I took the heaviest stone I could find;
And with one blow beat in its brains.

Ferret

More vicious than stoat or weasel
Because caged, kept hungry, the ferrets
Were let out only for the kill:
An alternative to sulphur and nets.

Once one, badly mauled, hid
Behind a treacle-barrel in the shed.
Throwing me back, Matthew slid
The door shut. From outside

The window, I watched. He stood
Holding an axe, with no gloves.
Then it sprang; and his sleeves
Were drenched in blood

Where the teeth had sunk. I hear
Its high-pitched squeal,
The clamp of its neat steel
Jaws. And I still remember

How the axe flashed, severing
The ferret's head,
And how its body kept battering
The barrels, long after it was dead.

In a Simple Light

Winter in this place
Is a tangerine sun.
Against the skyline
Nine Shetland ponies

Stand like cut-outs
Fraying at the edges.
Snow puffs and flurries
In weightless driblets

As they platter downhill,
Pink-hooved, chins
Stitched with frost, manes
Jiggling a tinsel trail.

They clutter and jolt,
Are pluff-bellied, biff
Posts, thrum their trough
With warm breathing, smelt

Ice. On the skyline
Again, part fancy, they
Freeze. In each eye
Is a tangerine sun.

On Craigie Hill

The farmhouse seems centuries ago,
The steadings slouched under a sifting of snow
For weeks on end, lamps hissing, logs stacked
Like drums in the shed, the ice having to be cracked
To let the shaggy cats drink. Or
Back from the mart through steaming pastures
Men would come riding – their best
Boots gleaming, rough tweeds pressed
To a knife-edge, pockets stuffed with notes.

Before that even, I could visualise (from coloured
Prints) traps rattling, wheels spinning; furred
Figures posing like sepia dolls
In a waxen world of weddings and funerals.
When Todd died, last of the old-stagers,
Friends of seventy years followed the hearse.
Soon the farm went out of the family: the Cochranes
Going to earth or, like their cousins,
Deciding it was time to hit town.

The last link broken, the farm-buildings stand
In a clutter below the quarry. The land
Retains its richness – but in other hands.
Kilmarnock has encroached. It is hard to look
Back with any sense of belonging.
Too much has changed, is still changing.
This blustery afternoon on Craigie Hill
I regard remotely the muddy track
My father used to trudge along, to school.

Farm

The sun drills the shire through and through
Till the farm is a furnace, the yard
A quivering wickerwork of flame. Pitchforks
Flash and fall. Bales are fiery ingots.
Straws sputter like squibs. Stones
Explode. From the byre, smack on time,
Old Martha comes clattering out
With buttered bannocks and milk in a pail.

Todd, his face ablaze, swims back
In what shadow there is. Hugh and John
Stretch out among sheaves. Hens squabble
For crusts; a dog flicks its tail
At a cleg; blueflies bunch like grapes.
Still the sun beats down, a hammer
On tin. And high overhead vapour-trails
Drift seaward, out past Ailsa Craig.

The Yard

The yard is littered with scrap, with axles
And tyres, buckled hoops and springs, all rusting.
The wreckage of cars that have been dumped.

The hut is still there. In the doorway
Two men talk horses – but not as he did
In the days when the Clydesdales came

To be shod, the milk-wagons for repair.
The din of iron on iron brings it all back:
Rob beating the anvil, to a blue flame.

The beast straining, the bit biting in,
Horn burning, the sour tang of iron,
The sizzling, the perfect fit of the shoe.

In his mind's eye, the whole yard is teeming
With horses, ducking blackthorn, tails
Swishing, the gates behind them clanging...

The men have started to strip an old van.
In passing he takes a kick at the wing. No one
Notices. The dead metal does not ring at all.

The Shed

When the milking was done, the byre
Mucked out, and the cows bedded
For the night, I would creep to the shed
Where the billy-goat was tethered

Behind the bales. His hooves danced
As we fought, striking sparks
As I swung him by the scruff or had him
By the beard, butting and kicking.

Now and then a whinny, as he shook himself
Free. His skull brick-hard, the eyes
Twists of straw. Or I'd force cow-cake
On him: his stench filling the shed.

The farm has changed hands twice.
Last week I visited it, the first
Time in years. As I passed the shed
A chain clanged – and I leapt aside

Suddenly terrified that the goat
(Or his wrinkled ghost) might come
Slithering over the straw-bales,
Pinning me back with his yellow eye.

Margins

It is one thing to talk of terror
In the abstract, quite another
To face up to the particular,
Fencing in the feeling of fear.

To speak, say, of a mother
Whose breast is touched by tumour;
Or the less explicit horror
Of a brother's mental disorder.

And most of all, in a rare
Moment, to explain to a daughter
What margins are: the nature
Of the charmed lives we bear.

Kilchrenan

Looking out on Cruachan, the church is whitewashed:
Monuments to McIntyre and McCorquedale

Kept simple, Cailean Mor's sword set in stone.
The old days would see some cold funerals.

As always, the gentry dominate. Two lofts
Used to face each other, where the lairds

Sat crossing glances, smouldering slowly
Under their ordered curls...the sermon droning.

See them descend, their ladies in lace,
Then jog arrogantly off, leaving behind

An odour of musk and Madeira, where now sheep
Go blindly nudging clumps of daffodils.

Crippled Aunt

As the sermon draws to a close, I glance
   Across at you through dusty chutes of light.
     The pews are golden. You sit
Padded with cushions, as in a trance:
Safe from the Devil and his vigorous dance.

Outside the bright world hums – no hive
   Brimming with honey, but traffic
     Bound for the coast. A truck
(Like the one that struck you?) drives
Past, stressing the miracle of your being alive.

You used to worship, on unbroken knees,
   In a village chapel with honeysuckle
     Ladling the air. I still
Have snapshots of you, among the roses.
God's will has strange ironies.

Such energy and gracefulness were yours
   It is baffling to see you sit
     Paralysed to the waist yet
Worshipping God who took your gay colours,
With a faith so elemental, fierce.

Watching them wheel you down the aisle, I am humble.
   I, who would curse the fate
     That has twisted you into what
You are, shudder to hear you say life's ample
For your needs, Christian by such example.

Craigie Hill

I once came across a pack of stoats in the sunlight,
Their eyes like jewels, the tips of their tails black.

One kept swinging on a fencepost and springing
To the ground, leaving the wires twanging.

As at a word of command, they took up
Close formation and moved off in one direction.

Knowing what I do now, I wouldn't have stood there
Watching, imagining them such dainty playthings.

Old Actor

Not the same nowadays. They don't play
Shakespeare properly – not the way
We used to. Too superior
For a frontcloth, that's their

Trouble. Opera use it, why not Theatre?
I mean, take the first scene from *Caesar* –
That ought to be done out front, the main
Area set for the procession.

As for *Hamlet*, a gravedigger here
Or there hardly matters any more.
(I saw Benson, as the Prince,
Carried off after 'The rest is silence' –

But that *improved* the text.) Donat,
Martin-Harvey...what *style*. Another thing,
We'd always an orchestra in the pit
For the Bard – not a gramophone in the wings.

Stage effects too: real waterfalls,
You name it – even Skegness,
Still the gas-floats. All they want these
Days in a lad is, well you know...*balls*.

Not that I'm against manliness,
Anything of the sort. Bawdry, for that matter.
I just think there are other
Things that count, besides filling a codpiece.

Birds of Passage

Why do we keep coming back, year
After year, who do not belong here?

To this rock, where black rabbits abound?
The soil is poor, the lighthouse unmanned.

There is nothing of birth, or possession.
Nor is it entirely the broch, with its sparse

Sward and saint's bones. Yet something stronger
Than mere habit (so unquestioned,

When the time comes) draws us to where
We can see the turnstone swoop, and hear

The mallard massing in the air.

Émigrée

A young girl in a faded photograph,
You sit delicately holding a fur muff:
Wistful yet wary, as though you already know
What winters await you, what habitual snow;
What unheated rooms and visits to the dacha
(Funeral bells tolling), what journeys on the Volga
In late spring, the pack-ice melting.

I imagine you trying out your halting
English on the servants; starting at a frown
On a familiar face, an icon staring down.
You are to escape all this, leaving behind
The women in black, the massive chambers
With their velvet curtains, the great chandeliers –
And outside, cannon firing along the frontiers
Of Europe. How you have changed over the years.

But I realise that what you have retained
Is a stunning sharpness of eye and mind.
Seeing through our masculine conjuring-tricks
A lesser concern, your ear is attuned
To the distant whistling of a more brutal axe.

Journeying North

Leaving Carlisle, the diesel pulls
Uphill, till a signal falls
And we put on speed.
                    That morning
I'd seen the Magritte exhibition
At the Tate. One portrait,
Of a couple kissing through sacking,
Put me in mind of Darnley
In his taffeta mask, then of our
Fumbling devotion.
                    Out there,
The slack reaches of Solway.

Another, more sinister,
Had two Edwardian figures
With a club and a net;
A nude on a bed,
Her mouth pouring blood.

Hurtling north, my fears
Are of a different order:
Imagining you laying my meal
On a frail cloth that might
Have been a bridal veil,
I consider the split cell,
The unruly corpuscle
In the gallery of the skull...

The air thick with tobacco-smoke
We near Gretna. Heavy anvils strike.

Driving through Sutherland

Here too the crofts were burned
To the ground, families stripped
And driven like cattle to the shore.
You can still hear the cursing,
The women shrieking.

                    The duke
And his lady sipped port, had
Wax in their ears. Thatch
Blazed. Thistles were torn up
By the root.

        There are men
In Parliament today who could
Be doing more.

           With these thoughts
In mind we drive from Overscaig
To Lairg, through a night as blue
As steel. Leaving Loch Shin behind
We find facing us an even colder
Firth, and a new moon rising
Delicately over a stubble field.

Summer Afternoon

She spends the afternoon in a deckchair,
Not moving, a handkerchief over
Her head. From the end of the garden
Her eyes look gouged. The children stare,
Then return to their game. She used to take
Them on country walks, or swimming in the lake.
These days are gone, and will not come again.

Dazzling slats of sunlight on the lawn
Make her seem so vulnerable; her bombazine
Costume fading with each drifting beam.
As the children squall, she imagines
Other generations: Is that you, Tom,
Or Ian, is it? – forgetting one was blown
To bits at Ypres, the other on the Somme.

Momentarily in pain, she tightens
Her lips into something like a grin.
There comes the first rustle of rain.
Carrying her in, you avoid my eye
For fear of interception, as who should say
Shall we, nearing extremity,
Be equal objects of distaste and pity?

Yet desperate in the meantime to forbear
For the sake of the love this poor
Creature bore us, who was once so dear.

North Uist
(for John Purser)

1

My new waders are like far-off dogs, whining.
My shoulder-strap could be a wheatear
Turning a corner. The wind, through the cleat
Of my landing-net, makes the squeaking
Of many mice busying themselves under cover.
On his ledge overlooking the loch
The buzzard that is too big for a buzzard
Eyes everything stonily, then takes his pick.

2

Uist, a smashed mirror.
I holiday here,
To gather strength for the winter.
So I fire my peats, gut
Trout, rub cold hands together:
Reassured that when December
Does come, I shall be far
From here. Like all city dwellers.

3 *Solas*

I try to locate a tiny ratchet
At my right ear, an insomniac
Cheese-grater somewhere beyond my toes.
The place is hoaching with mice. They are in
For the winter. Every so often
We have an eyeball to eyeball confrontation.
One way to dispose of them is to fire
The thatch. A costly operation.

4 *Sgurr an Duin*

Three days I have trudged
After a pair of eagles; sighting them
Occasionally, overhead or on fence-stakes,

Surveying their land. This evening,
Probing gobbets of fur, disgorged bone,
I am perceived by a deer who stands sniffing,
Then bounds over the wire,
And effortlessly away.

5

Striding back from the Co-op, I clutch
My sodden groceries in a plastic bag
One handle of which is sprung.
Proud of the buffeting
I'm taking, I feel I belong:
Till I meet a chained mongrel,
Yap-yapping; and an old woman
Who slurches past, head down.

6   *Vallay Strand*

The sky consists of strips
Of blue, like a holiday postcard.
I sit writing, like a man writing
A holiday postcard. The strips
Turn to steel, to smoky grey.
The tide recedes, and recedes,
All the way to Vallay. Meanwhile,
The multitudinous sandworms turn and turn.

7

If, as the pundits say,
A new Ice Age does
Come, well I suppose Uist
Will be as ready as most.
The skuas sharp as razors;
The lochans, crystal.
And in the long chambers,
The War Lords are sleeping still.

Three Circus Poems

Lion-Tamer

So, the hot breath, the ring round me
Of haunch and mane, the eye always on me.
Strop of muscular shoulder, the easy
Stride, tail switching the sawdust up.
The jaws foremost in my mind – which take
Flesh, drip flame: could at no notice
A man's sinews snap, like a clown
Draw me tattered through a paper hoop.

Not skill, but knowledge. Of the fiery
Bowl, the fierce flower that's lion.
Attention caught. The soft paw. Giant
Cat. Who's met, who's held, who's master.
The one danger (and lion can sense it)
That the mind slip from its ring
To where the crowd sits, tier upon tier,
Its breath fetid, hungering for the killing.

Clown

Week in, week out, over half England. Folk
Laughing their ruddy heads off. My world
A paper hoop, coloured balls, a plastic
Smile. Beginning to get past it, though.
Mean to say, it knocks me out. You try
Being up a ladder one minute, the next flat
On your face. Fancy a turn on the stilts?
Or having cold water squirted up your pants?

Okay for the seven-and-sixes. But how
About me? My eyes itching, gut stuck
With straw, sweat in my armpits pricking.
What you could call scratching a living.
Had a couple of goes at the telly: interviewed,
And that. Ruined my chances, ask me.
'This bloke you're always on about' I said,
'This bloke Hamlet – who the ruddy hell's he?'

Elephant-Girl

Like I keep trying to tell you, just
An ordinary girl. This maharanee
Stuff, that's strictly for the show...
Yes, Shettleston, my mum tells me.
The usual tastes, what do you mean?
The leather gear's for the act, see.
That's right, the boots too. Look
Ducky, there's nothing kinky about me.

The circus? No choice. Born into it,
Like I said. In the blood. Talk
And breathe elephants. Sat
On their backs before I could walk...
That's right, develops the muscles.
Could be dangerous, I suppose. Never think
About it. Elephants is like people, you see:
Okay, so long as you can take the stink.

B

Tutorial

'Leaving aside Fielding's peculiarly national
Style, let us trace the novel

Through Miss Austen: observation
Allied to wit, a feminine intuition…'

With pleasing prejudice and pride
We take a cabriolet-ride

Down sunny lanes (bypassing Thackeray,
And Scott's drayhorse, on the way).

Tempting though it is to drink in
The country setting, the formal scenes,

I keep seeing those metal wheels spin –
And a young girl, composed, holding the reins.

Forbears

My father's uncle was the fastest
Thing on two wheels, sitting in a gig,
The reins tight, his back at an angle
Of thirty degrees, puffing up dust-clouds
As he careered down Craigie Hill.

His father before him, the strongest man
In Ayrshire, took a pair of cartwheels
By the axle and walked off with them. I have
Visions of him in the meadow, holding
Two ropes, a stallion straining on each.

Before that, no doubt, we boasted
The straightest furrow, the richest yield.
No measurement needed: each farm
Bore its best, as each tree its fruit.
We even had a crazy creature in crinolines

Who locked her letters in a brass box.
Others too... But what do such truths
Add up to – when the nearest
(And furthest) I get is visiting
Their elaborate, uncared-for graves?

On an adjoining stone are a skull
And hourglass, from Covenanter
Days. Their lives were a duller
Sacrifice. John on his moral staff,
The great-aunts with their rigid ways,

Smacking of goodness in the strictest
Sense, members of a sect, Elect almost,
Shared surely something of flint
In the brain. Sad, that their mortal goal
Was salvation, not purification of the soul.

Farm Funeral

His hearse should have been drawn by horses.
That's what he envisaged: the strain
And clop of crupper and chain, flashing
Brass, fetlocks forcing high. With below
Him, the frayed sheets turning slowly yellow.

On the sideboard a silver cup he had won,
Inscribed 'to Todd Cochrane', now a lamp;
And tinted prints of his trotting days,
Switch in hand, jockey-capped, the gig silky
With light, wheels exquisitely spinning.

For fifty years he was a breeder of horses;
Nursing them nightly, mulling soft praise
Long after the vet would have driven his plunger in.
Yet through them was his hip split. Twice
He was crushed by a stallion rearing.

Himself to the end unbroken. God's tool, yes,
That to earth will return. But not before time.
He ought to have been conveyed to the grave
By clattering Clydesdales, not cut off
From lark and sorrel by unseemly glass.

The shire is sprinkled with his ashes.
The fields are green through his kind. Their clay,
His marrow. As much as the roisterer, he: even
That last ride to Craigie, boots tightly laced,
His tie held in place by a diamond pin.

II.

The Chinese Tower

I

Hard land and dry, yet already
The lavender-clumps are bristling
Like hassocks for Provençal ladies.

Crickets cross and uncross their legs.
The pine-slopes are musty. Soon
The valley will turn as on a spit.

In this world of bells, of goats
Heavily thonged, of thyme tracking
The tree-line, so single-minded

Do the senses become that for them
The only escape is trussed brutally
To the bellies of great beasts.

II

But under rain, the land
Is tin. There is brimstone
Among the mountains.

Watertroughs overflow
Like basins of wine.
Lightning fills the street.

Then two men with umbrellas
And between them
Fifty sheep whose bells

Are the din of a drowned
City. Now they are gone.
The crickets, too, are silent.

III

In as never before such blueness
(Though to them the merest
Translation of summer) two huntsmen

Traverse the valley. They tack
As one, as yachts evenly paced;
Though here in no breeze, but welter

Of blueness. Even time can be treated
In terms of colour: nor arises
Matter of identity. The cricket's

Disguise, the butterfly fired
From slate – these are proof,
Not part, of the same. You doubt it?

Watch then those huntsmen
Scouring that hill. Watch them
Halt, as one. Watch an arm

Rise, and fall. And wait,
The length of the valley away,
For the sound of rushing stone.

IV

Or I find you, in a straw hat,
Chasing butterflies. Even they
Stress the one-ness of it all,

Whose every movement is irretrievable
Yet infinitely repeated. Such
Is the truth not of this place only

But of things – hence of things
In this place. A bluetail shimmers
In a specific, no mere casual sun.

V

The waters of a mountain stream
Assume the shape of ravine, then
Create ravines of their own

In air. This in accordance
With the natural freedom
Of things. And the village pump

Always runs, a silver thread.
Ravine and rich chasm in one,
Its surface is a source of light.

VI

In a wilderness that is
No wilderness but a pasture
Among pines, the shepherd

Has built his cabin. Between
The sources of light and water.
There is much philosophy in this.

His pack always holds
Hypodermics against viper-bite.
For the sheep, not himself.

For himself there is a stick.
Nor does he waste time deducing
What is there clearly to be seen.

VII

At a given moment, there may
Be no scent, no sign
Of fox: no instant indication.

Thus the jays go cackling
From thicket to thicket, consumed
With pride. Yet remains

Always presence of fox.
The air where he has been
Holds his shape...

VIII

High among pines, on a hill
Overlooking the chapel, is a Chinese
Tower. Both in name, and style.

Behind it a viper lies coiled.
Is he lord of this place?
Has he an enquiring mind?

But the pines change from green
To smoky blue. Already there is
A chill in the air. Questions

Need no answer. In absence,
The presence of snake grows
Strangely stronger. This square

Of stone: an outlook tower.
Yet from few places can it be seen.
Certainly from nowhere in the village.

IX

Of the tower three things
Are commonly said. That
At its base is a well

Of pure water (this being
Open to proof). That formerly
A tunnel led underground

To the village (this
To be taken on trust).
And thirdly that once,

In time of fire, monks
Went dripping like candle-wax
Down the face of the rock.

X

From the Chinese tower can be seen
The swerve of the valley, the lavender
Fields and the mountains, pink

Beyond. With finger in air
You can trace the tracks
Of ravines, mark the pantiled

Roofs of houses, of lofts, of the church
That strikes every hour twice.
And slowly, the blueness becomes

Penetrable. There must always
Be just such a place – its
Tiny bells chinking in the wind.

[*Thorame, Provence*]

Tremors

We took turns at laying
An ear on the rail –
So that we could tell
By the vibrations

When a train was coming.
Then we'd flatten ourselves
To the banks, scorched
Vetch and hedge-parsley,

While the iron flanks
Rushed past, sending sparks
Flying. It is more and more
A question of living

With an ear to the ground:
The tremors, when they come,
Are that much greater –
For ourselves, and others.

Nor is it any longer
A game, but a matter
Of survival: each explosion
Part of a procession

There can be no stopping.
Though the end is known,
There is nothing for it
But to keep listening.

A Sense of Order

Sunday Walk

I stop at the foot of Garioch Drive
Where my aunt used to live
Three floors up.
              I remember the smell
Of camomile that hit you in the hall,
The embroidered sampler, the jars
Of wax chrysanths, the budgerigars
In their lacquered cage; the ladies who came
To read the Bible in the front room –
Surrounded by marzipan, and dragons
On silky screens.
              A rag-and-bone man,
His pony ready for the knacker's yard,
Rounds a corner (short of a tail-light)
And disappears up Clouston Street.

Below, the Kelvin runs like stinking lard.

Period Piece

Hand in hand, the girls glide
Along Great Western Road.
                   Outside
The Silver Slipper the boys wait,
Trousers flared, jacket-pockets
Bulging with carry-outs.

The girls approach. A redhead pouts,
Sticks her tongue out,
Then passes under the strung lights
To the dance-floor. 'I'll have it
Off with that one.' 'Want to bet?'
'I'd rather lumber her mate...'

They nick their cigarettes.
                  Inside,
The miniskirts are on parade,
Listening to The Marmalade.

Cranworth Street

I climb the tenement stair
With its scoured tiles, its odour
Of cat.
      We lived here, before
My father moved to Ayrshire.
I have not been back, for years.

The brass nameplate, the square
Bellpull, mean nothing any more.
What is there to recapture,
To rediscover? It is too late
In the season, for that.

I cling to the wooden
Rail and, for no reason,
Break out in a sweat
As I reach the street.

Street Scene

The faces outside the Curlers
Explode like fat cigars
In the frosty air.

Even the newspaper-seller
Rocks on his heels, half-seas over.
And I don't blame him.

      As the pictures
Come out, scores of lovers
Head for their parked cars.

Two ladies whisper
Goodnight to each other.
Neither feels secure
Till on her own stair
She snibs the basement door
And breathes freely, behind iron bars.

Family Visit

Laying linoleum, my father spends hours
With his tape measure,
Littering the floor
As he checks his figures, gets
The angle right; then cuts
Carefully, to the music
Of a slow logic. In despair
I conjure up a room where
A boy sits and plays with coloured bricks.

My mind tugging at its traces,
I see him in more dapper days
Outside the Kibble Palace
With my grandfather, having
His snapshot taken; men firing
That year's leaves.
The Gardens are only a stone's throw
From where I live...But now
A younger self comes clutching at my sleeve.

Or off to Innellan, singing, we would go,
Boarding the steamer at the Broomielaw
In broad summer, these boomps-a-daisy
Days, the ship's band playing in a lazy
Swell, my father steering well clear
Of the bar, mother making neat
Packets of waste-paper to carry
To the nearest basket or (more likely)
All the way back to Cranworth Street.

Leaving my father at it
(He'd rather be alone) I take
My mother through the changed Botanics.
The bandstand is gone, and the great
Rain-barrels that used to rot
And overflow. Everything is neat
And plastic. And it is I who must walk
Slowly for her, past the sludge
And pocked granite of Queen Margaret Bridge.

To My Father

One of my earliest memories (remember
Those Capone hats, the polka-dot ties)
Is of the late thirties: posing
With yourself and grandfather before
The park railings; me dribbling
Ice cream, you so spick and smiling
The congregation never imagined
How little you made. Three generations,
In the palm of a hand. A year later
Grandfather died. War was declared.

In '42 we motored to Kilmarnock
In Alec Martin's Terraplane Hudson.
We found a pond, and six goldfish
Blurred under ice. They survived
That winter, but a gull got them in the end.
Each year we picnicked on the lawn;
Mother crooking her finger
As she sipped her lime. When
They carried you out on a stretcher
She knew you'd never preach again.

Since you retired, we've seen more
Of each other. Yet I spend this forenoon
Typing, to bring you closer – when
We could have been together. Part of what
I dread is that clear mind nodding
Before its flickering screen. If we come over
Tonight, there will be the added irony
Of proving my visit isn't out of duty
When, to myself, I doubt the dignity
Of a love comprising so much guilt and pity.

Reiteration

What terrifies me is that you should see your death
Reflected in my eyes. Yours are moist, glazed
Over; rimmed with red, as you gaze
At the images on their tiny screen. Beneath

The surface of things, your heart takes
Irregular leaps forward, toward the dark.
Its rhythms are broken easily; by the van parked
Too close for comfort, the fool whose brakes

Took him through the Argyle Street
Lights; Lennox's goal in the dying minutes...
And I think of the pressures youth puts
On age, neither prepared to meet

The other half-way. I remember you beat
Me, with a leather belt, for using a word
That can nowadays be overheard
Even in your trim Bearsden street.

I swore I'd get my own back
When I was older, stronger:
I'd wait till you no longer
Had the upper hand, and give you an attack

One way or another. Now I see
How strengths vary; the grasp
Of one over another depending not on the clasp
Of wrist or forearm. You are still stronger than me –

And apart from all else, have more experience
Of death's ways, having watched others go.
Here in this tiny space, you
Stare calmly at what I only dimly sense.

Far from being imprisoned in this room,
Which is how I'd seen it, the big guns
Thudding, I realise you've won
More battles than most – and have just one to come.

Choral Symphony

The customary conversation
Gives way to applause
For the Orchestra. Then
A roar, as Karajan
Takes the stand. He raises
His baton: the strings swoop in.

During the interval, we remain
Seated. Two Edinburgh ladies
Behind us complain:
'Such Teutonic discipline
Breeds perfection,
Not Art.' Their companion agrees.

At the end they join in,
As the ovation goes on
And on. What has changed their tune?
We overhear: 'Weren't the Chorus
Superb!' 'As one voice.'
'And that lace, on Muriel's dress.'

In the Kibble Palace

In the Kibble Palace with its dazzling statues
And glass dome, reading a poet I've just come across,
I learn that under ice the killer whale

Seeing anything darker than snow, falls away
Then charges, smashing the ice with his forehead,
Isolating seal or man on a drifting piece

Of the floe. Imagine those tons of blubber
Thrusting up; tail curveting
As the hammer head hits. What if the skull

Should split, splinters penetrate to the brain?
Nor will dry land protect us from the thudding
In the blood, these forces below. How can we conquer

Who cannot conquer ourselves? I shall think of this
When, fishing on frosted glass, I find
My line tightening against the swell;

Or hearing you moan and turn in your sleep
I know you are on your own, far out,
Dark shapes coursing below. Meanwhile

The horizon closes in, a glass
Globe. We will admit it is there
When it is too late; and blunder for the exits

To find them locked. Seeing as though through ice
Blurred forms gyrate, we will put our heads
Together and try to batter a way out.

Aldridge Pond

To this salt-water enclosure
Came families of fin-whales,
Anything up to eighty tons, superior
In hunting method to our sonar.
Turning their underbellies to the light
They'd herd the herring closer and closer
Then take what food they wanted.
Till one January, the herring in glut,
A pregnant mother-whale entered
An inlet she could not have navigated
But for the spring tide. Her mate,
Unable to join her, drove shoal upon shoal
Into the pool where she had been caught.
What a chance for the conservationists,
The marine biologists. Their help never
Came. After four days 400 nickel bullets
Were bedded in her body; a motor-boat's blade
Had cut a swath from her side. The fishermen
Saw in her perhaps an exemplar
Of their own servitude. Some wanted
To preserve her till the height
Of the tourist season. None ministered
To the sores that finally festered.

They towed her, by the tail, out to sea
Where she floated easily, borne
By the gases of her own dissolution.

At Coruisk

1

Think of it: a honeymoon at the foot
Of the Cuillin, and not once to see them
For mist – till on the last day we broached
From Elgol the seven crowned kings.

So intense the experience: not summers only,
But years, cramming one afternoon –
Thus keenly the glimpse awaited.
Nor had been envisaged such blueness:

Ice-crests mirrored in Coruisk, blue
Upon blue, as we followed
The path home. The moon crescent.
The sky, powdered flint.

2

Tempting to see these things
As manifestations of the mind
Significant through ourselves,
Which precede and succeed our notice.

For all that, the shadows are real.
They darken or illumine, at will;
Are points from which
To examine ourselves. But watch

How you go: yonder are scurrs
Would cut you down; nearer
To hand, rusty bracken,
Peat-holes where you'd cramp and drown.

3

So we get to know landscape,
And each other, better;
Our breathing filling the air
With each lap tackled. We learn

That the end of the road is seldom
A given point; that bridges exist
Too narrow to be crossed
More than two abreast.

Yet remains the fear, when
We look round, that two figures
Not dissimilar to ourselves should appear
Transparent, then vanish altogether.

Marriage a Mountain Ridge

1

Like most, one way or another, ours
Has been through some dark couloirs.

I cannot swear to actual crevasses –
But have sensed them underfoot. (One night

On Beinn Fhada I lost my footing, and was fortunate
A rowan took my weight.)

This way I am better equipped
For keeping, if not to the spirit, the letter.

Crampons and pitons fitted, we face
The next assault, roped together. I also carry

An ice-pick – but fear to use it,
Lest it sink too deeply in.

2

Perhaps the hardest lesson
Is to accept the Brocken,

The Man with the Rainbow, as stemming
From myself; a projection

Of my own form. The cauldron
Below me, thin air.

In these rarified labyrinths
The way forward

Is to focus
On a fixed point;

One hand gripping firmly
Its moral thread.

3

Whether scaling Etive
Of the shifting faces,

Or on the summit of Blaven,
Sheet-ice glistening

Through walls of mist,
It is all one. The tracks

We pursue are ours;
The zone we would enter

Not the mountains, but ourselves.
So for a moment, the mind

May afford to swing out
Over the wide abyss.

4

Then comes the point when body
And mind are one, each indefinable

Except in terms of the other.
Head and heart held

In a single noose. The Beast,
The Grey Man, cannot touch us here.

His footprints descending,
Identical with our own.

Later, victims of Time and Loss,
We will return and gaze there –

And marvel at such heights
Conquered, such blazing air.

After the Party

I drive you home.
Your seat-belt fastened
To take you in. Your time
Draws near. Never
Have I seen on you such a bloom.

Fears skim
The surface. Most
Remain unspoken. Now
And again though,
We talk the next stage through.

The car garaged, I follow
You in. Loaded with gifts
We've been given.
Who survive by moving
From one house of glass to another.

Under the Ice

Like Coleridge, I waltz
on ice. And watch my shadow
on the water below. Knowing that
if the ice were not there
I'd drown. Half willing it.

In my cord jacket
and neat cravat, I keep
returning to the one spot.
How long, to cut
a perfect circle out?

Something in me
rejects the notion.
The arc is never complete.
My figures-of-eight
almost, not quite, meet.

Was Raeburn's skating parson
a man of God, poised
impeccably on the brink;
or his bland stare
no more than a decorous front?

If I could keep my cool
like that. Gazing straight ahead,
not at my feet. Giving
no sign of knowing
how deep the water, how thin the ice.

Behind that, the other
question: whether the real you
pirouettes in space,
or beckons from under the ice
for me to come through.

'Kitchen-Maid'

Reaching the Rijksmuseum
mid-morning, in rain,
we skirt the main hall
with its tanned
tourists and guides

and, ignoring the rooms
we saw yesterday,
find ourselves heading
past Avercamp's skaters,
Brueghel's masses of flowers,

and even the Night-Watch
in its noisy arena
till, up carpeted stairs,
we are in a chamber
made cool by Vermeer.

For what might be hours
we stand facing
a girl in a blue apron
pouring milk
from a brown jug.

Time comes to a stop.
Her gesture will stay
perpetually in place.
The jug will never empty,
the bowl never fill.

It is like seeing
a princess
asleep, under ice.
Your hand, brushing mine,
sustains the spell:

as I turn to kiss you,
we are ourselves
suspended in space;
your appraising glance
a passionate embrace.

Visiting Hour

In the pond of our new garden
were five orange stains, under
inches of ice. Weeks since anyone
had been there. Already by far
the most severe winter for years.
You broke the ice with a hammer.
I watched the goldfish appear,
blunt-nosed and delicately clear.

Since then so much has taken place
to distance us from what we were.
That it should come to this.
Unable to hide the horror
in my eyes, I stand helpless
by your bedside and can do no more
than wish it were simply a matter
of smashing the ice and giving you air.

Arrivals

1

The plane meets
its reflection on the wet
runway, then crosses
to where I wait
behind plate glass.

I watch
with a mixture
of longing and despair
as you re-enter
the real world.

All we have is each other.
I sometimes wonder
if that is enough;
whether being together
enlarges or diminishes grief.

2

Remember arriving
from Thorame –
the scent
of honey,
of lavender clinging.

On the Jonte,
climbing goat-tracks
to drink from a spring
under an arch
of red sandstone.

Or last year,
a second honeymoon
in Amsterdam, having
exchanged gifts: a miniature
war-horse, a silver ring.

3

Tonight your return
from Ulster
renders
my fears unfounded.
Yet neither

of us speaks. Instead
we think of those
living there, others
who have died.
Your brother-in-law

has decided to emigrate:
the one sure escape.
As I draw up
at the lights, you droop
forward, hands on your lap.

4

The pubs are coming out.
In Dumbarton Rd
two drunks, having battered
each other senseless, sit
in their own vomit.

No one interferes.
It is not easy
to accept there may
be a certain mercy
in living here.

The lights turn
to green. I imagine
you lying alone
in a white room, surrounded
by flimsy screens...

Bonfire

Relations are strained, again, with next door.
This morning the oldest boy, having broken
One of my wife's favourite shrubs, got
The rough edge of my tongue. (Any
Day now, they'll have the wall down.)

So as I light the bonfire, instead of the usual
Clutter of children twirling burning paper,
The only acknowledgement is the twitch
Of curtains, scowls from behind the pane.
I stack the twigs, pile the dry leaves on.

Soon I am aware of another preoccupation.
Every twenty minutes, a different gentleman
Comes from next door; followed shortly after
By a blue-skirted girl, who brings another back.
Slow on the uptake (this being a respectable

Neighbourhood) it is only later I realise
She must be on the game. To bring up children
Here. I am sickened by a mixture of smoke
And desire. You call that tea is ready.
I run for the door, leaving the rake lying.

Very late, I go out to check the bonfire.
Two figures move, in the shadow. A radio
Blares. A light on the first floor
Cuts through scarlet curtains. Where
My heaps of leaves had been, grey embers glow.

Passion Fruit

'This is the genuine site of the Garden of Eden.'
Who are we, to doubt it? The guide drones on.
'Eve's apple, at least, proffers no problem:
Contemplate, if you will, the passion-flower fruit.'

Persuasive enough, in the fragrant gloom.
A rustling at the glade's cool rim
Conveys the serpent's progress. 'As your party
Leaves, you will receive gifts of passion fruit.'

Despite the light's apparent purity,
Not one of my transparencies came out.
And at Los Angeles, on my flight
Home, they confiscated the passion fruit.

Aquarium

Fishes striped like spinnakers
Bob toward us, then blousily
Go about. Theirs is a dark
World, haunted by bubbles.
Tapping the glass does nothing

To distract them, their steady
Intake. Press your face to it,
They merely distort further.
It is as though we were peering
Through a two-way mirror;

Underwater voyeurs, taking
The tide's pulse as well
As our own. Is this
How it will begin –
When the glaciers melt

And the caves refill?
How it will all end,
As we wait for the kill?
A face is imprinted
On the glass. An attendant,

Seeming scarcely to breathe,
Switches out the lights.
Luminous fronds unfurl.
Still no sound. Your ringed
Hand comes against mine, clutching.

At Amersham
(for Kay)

Entering the chapel, you survey
for a moment your husband's coffin.
He is gone; after an illness
made less hideous by the devotion
shown in its face. Your coat is green,
his colour. On your wedding-finger
the matching ring from Amsterdam,
where you spent your honeymoon
two years ago. There comes a kind of trembling.
Like a young bride, you walk down
the aisle. The lovelorn bouquets loom.

*

The curtain is closed, the benediction
said. We come out, into the sun.

Your black limousine accelerates down the drive.
Grief is poised in the air, the crest of a wave.

*

In my mind's
eye, I keep
seeing a stretch
of bare beach;
on it, the wind
howling, a reed that bends —

and will not snap.

C

Night Incident

Three nights running
you have wakened crying:

this time, because you heard
footsteps in your bedroom cupboard.

How do I help you understand
beyond

saying they are
from next door?

You calm down,
ask to see the moon.

It is full, tonight.
As we look out

I think of a lifetime
of haunted rooms,

of the violence
that is your inheritance.

I carry
you carefully

upstairs, and put
you in your cot;

then tiptoe to the door.
Your breathing is there, and no more.

Ghosts

My face against the bars
of your cot, close to yours,

I listen while you whisper
urgently, telling me where

you want to go. Needless
to say, it is the Kibble Palace.

As soon as you are dressed
and have had breakfast

we set off; a fine
mist rising from the Kelvin.

We are alone in the Gardens.
Leaving the pram at the entrance

I take you to where the goldfish are.
For what seems hours, you peer

through the murky
water. Under the lattice-work

of white spars, whose
curved glass has

mirrored family upon family,
we too shall soon be,

like my father and grandfather,
ghosts in the empty air.

Afternoon Visit

It is a gusty April afternoon.
  The wrestling is on television,
Punctuated by adverts. Her walking, even
  This past week, has slowed down

Perceptibly, her leg grown stiffer.
  At one point, getting up
  To adjust the set, she overbalances. Before
Either of us can intervene, a cup

And saucer fall to the floor.
  Neither breaks. What does snap,
Surprisingly, is her composure.
  Taking her grandchild on her lap

She strokes his head over and again,
  Not noticing the tears
Flow. 'Love is the main
  Thing. Yet let Nature take its course.

Children are their own. Time must come,
  It cannot be helped.' And strokes
That helpless head. I remember at home
  Sitting on her lap, surrounded by books

And ornaments bought over the years,
  Most of them to be chipped, at least,
By ourselves as children. 'There's
  No evading it...' Some fearful beast

Within me refuses to listen; would smash
  Down the walls, the watercolours
In their frames; the precious trash
  Of a lifetime. I am no longer hers,

She is saying – not knowing it
  But speaking simply, without grievance,
From the heart. How can I be fit
  To raise children, I wonder; tense

With foreboding on their behalf and my own,
  Who am already a father before
Having learned to be a son.
  The child slips lightly to the floor

And plays there. Her eyes mist
  Over. I concentrate on the faded green
Of an apron. What will become of us, at the last?
  Men fight through blizzards, on the TV screen.

The Lilypond

I stand at the edge of the lilypond
With its swart fronds
And submerged stems. Scarcely defined
Forms nudge the surface and dip back down.

Years ago, I seem to remember, the water
Was clear; the leaves green saucers
You wanted to walk on. Beyond,
The hot-house. Now its spars

Are smashed, the iron flamingoes
Gone. One day soon, the pond
Is to be drained. I shall not be here.
Better simply arrive and find

The area filled in, than see
The process as I imagine it:
Orange shapes with white
Growths being scooped out

By men in rubber gloves;
Then speedily disposed of.
I'd be free to surmise
The stench, the bunches of flies.

In so many ways, we avoid
Being in at the death;
Preferring to let nature take its course,
And putting in an appearance

When we know all is safe.
Again and again I am drawn
Here, to the lilypond.
Elsewhere, there is hurt enough.

Along the Terrace

Drinks, along the Terrace.

Another marriage, it appears,
Is on the slide. Neither party
Has anything to hide.

                       Are we
Merely waiting our turn?

                       In bed
That night, we lie so close
It is impossible to tell
Whose is the jumping pulse.

To the Bear Park

Forgetting it was Bank Holiday Monday
I headed for Loch Lomond; wondering why
The roads were so crowded. Eventually,
Seeing 'to the Bear Park', something
I'd not normally fancy, we went in.

The car in front was jammed with children.
Ignoring notices prohibiting open
Windows, they leaned out, patting
Frayed fur as brown bears explored
The bonnet and came nuzzling at the running-board.

When the warden asked the driver to move on,
All he got was abuse. As soon as he'd gone,
Down came the windows again. I imagined
The headline: 'Young children
Mauled'; underneath, between portions

Of flesh, the father's lumpish grin.
Looking sideways at you
I wonder how often I wind
Equivalent windows, blindly, down. Iron
Gates open. We drive, slowly, through.

Seize the Day

Come on daddy, come now I hear them shout
As I put the finishing touches to this and that

In the safe confines of my study:
Hurry daddy before it's too late, we're ready!

They are so right. Now is the time.
It won't wait, on that you can bet your bottom

Dollar. So rouse yourself, get the drift
Before you're muffled and left

For useless. *Let's build a snow-man, then
A snow-woman to keep him company. When*

*That's finished, and with what's left over,
A giant snow-ball that will last for ever,*

Only hurry daddy. A soon as this poem
Is finished, I promise, I'll come –

Essential, first, to pin down what is felt.
Meanwhile the snow begins to melt.

Removal

Where are they from, half these things
Heaped about me? What doors have been forced,
What cupboards cleared, the first time in years?
Have I seen that photo-album, ever before?

These prints? Do I remember
Those catalogues, from the Galleries
Of whose youth? That vase, did we not *notice*?
This mildewed rucksack, how come *it* is here?

Through extending rows of poplars, I see
A bare slope; a young couple climbing there.
In Provence perhaps: swallow-tails swooping,
Thyme in the air. Or the steps of some monastery

In a shaded land...the hour striking.
Each memory, as it clarifies, happy
Yet packed with pain. The light hardens.
I hear your foot, upon the attic stair.

III. NEW POEMS

Moving In

October ends. Against my study wall
the rose-hips shrivel. The central

heating is like leaves shifting
behind the skirting.

The boys' woollens and long stockings
are laid out for the morning.

Since the hour went back there has been
mist, incessant rain.

At dusk the New Town
comes into its own:

a cat at each corner, shady permutations
of wives and lovers gliding through its lanes.

In bed, we cling to one another
and prepare for a long winter.

Autumn Crocuses

I walk through the Botanic Garden.
Usually the children are there, alert
In the sun, feeding the squirrels peanuts
Or running to hide among the rhododendrons.

It is strange without them, as though
They were already grown up and gone:
The way it will be, before long – who
However much they belong, are their own.

Through my dark glasses, tree-trunks gleam
Like stanchions in a still pool. Among layers
Of mulch leaves, autumn crocuses bloom
Blue as gentians...their stems slender.

Birthday

At a quarter to six he comes pattering
Through to our room, asking can he unwrap
His presents. Most are in coloured paper,
Sellotaped together. Excitement has no bounds

As he flits from package to package, lays out
His new draughts pieces, the triangle
From my mother, rustles through the tissue
For what he may have missed. Since midnight,

He says, he has been five. Brilliant, under
The centre light, he touches the heart.
Outside, in another murderous
Dawn, the world prises itself apart.

Penicuik House

Of eleven bays comprising the front façade,
Three advance to support a pediment
On which a slender steeple-clock is mounted.
To the rear, as a doocot, a Roman victory monument.

In the interior, charred chimney-pieces;
A pair of oak pedestals flanking a mirror
Rescued from the old house:
The two buildings confronting each other

Across azalea beds, this fragrant afternoon.
And see, the photographs in the billiard-room
Of smoke billowing from the ruined mansion;
Foreground figures, in Victorian costume,

Elegantly reclining – their casualness
In the face of destruction so incongruous
As to seem surreal. The explanation:
Having saved all they could before the roof caved in,

Protection from the sun, that blazing day in June,
Was the next consideration. Only in imagination,
Those smoke-wisps across sepia features,
Before each girl, and parasol, mercilessly flares.

At the Hairdresser

Behind white astragals, I sit
Waiting to have my hair cut.
Soon it will flounce, a greying frazzle, at my feet;
The face in the mirror, sharply lit,
Resembling mine, but with more lines
Than I'd care to acknowledge, deeply slit
Into the features as by theatre make-up.

All round, women flit – as though part
Of some Japanese ritual: brown-smocked,
Hair rolled, silent as steam rises
And water swirls and plops
In each dazzling sink. Resorting to no tricks
Of rejuvenescence, I face facts;
Ask simply that it be trimmed, not too short.

On glass-topped tables *Cosmopolitan* and *She*,
Sheer gloss, assist in the process
Of holding time, momentarily, at bay.
As the scissors snip, I become conscious
Of plants in their pots, smooth leaves polished
On the surface but each underside frayed,
Marking the tiny red spiders' unyielding progress.

Snowfall

Slow thaw

Slabs of snow, stacked against the guttering,
Keel on the lip, then slop down
On the tarrea tubs littering
The area. Each clearance brings
Filthy water, as from a gushet;
A juddering of clogged veins.
We switch off television, sit
Watching nothing. Each of us wonders what
To say. Tomorrow we shall have the great
Thaw to discuss. Meanwhile there is tonight.

Mid-week

'Like felled logs' you say. And 'Yes, the alarm
Has gone, did you not hear?' A small child charms
Us with 'Open the shutters, so I can see out.'
The mind wallowing from last night's
Trough, I go through. The rutted snow
Has gone to slush, not frozen. Along the Row
Cars start. People pass, looking in.
I switch off the centre light. Our bin
Is on the pavement, on its side,
Its lid gone. Is there nothing we can hide?

Japanese bowl

They are bringing the dead off the mountain.
It has been the worst winter for years.
You ask, can we go sledging. In the Gardens
Yesterday a father sat his small daughter,
Shrieking with laughter, on a new toboggan,
Then watched helpless as it careered
Downhill into a tree. I still hear
The crack of her skull – and cannot tear
My eyes from this glazed Japanese
Bowl, its surface minutely crazed.

D

Spoilage

After a fortnight, snow is no longer
A novelty. The drop in temperature
Has made a rink of Ann Street. More

Than old ladies teeter. The children
Give up looking for dragons'
Footprints, having found none.

It seems an age since the world was clean
And we went sledging in the Gardens.
Now any pretence at purity has gone:

In my heavy coat, and since last night
Nursing a chipped humerus, I concentrate
On skirting ice patches and areas of dogshit.

Sorley Maclean

Some poets erect edifices
    Simple or baroque in accordance
With taste; then with ice
    Pick and pitons, do a dance

On the sheer face. Others
    Thrive underwater;
Pot-holers, skin-divers
    For sunken treasure.

Your rareness lies in
    Out-doing these; who conquer
The princely Cuillin,
    Plumb the chill of Morar.

Against both you pit
    Yourself ultimately
To preserve love's heartbeat
    In the face of eternity.

And I think of Lear
    On the edge of the abyss,
So tenderly aware
    Of human helplessness.

Pentland Poems

Above Glencorse

In the lee of a stunted pine, we pour
Coffee from a thermos, adding whisky
To keep out the chill. Perched here
It is hard to escape from history.

Vigorous on the summit of Castlelaw
Scott would tell of Covenanters
Joyless on the sward below.
Earlier, startled worshippers

Watched highland soldiery swagger
Towards Holyrood; the Young Pretender,
Unaware of Derby, impending Culloden,
Flicking at flies with a blotched cane.

Breathing deeply, the air keen,
I keep thinking of Stevenson
Longing for home. How soon,
In some Samoa of our own,

Will we sense the grim-visaged visitor come
And, peering through time,
Wonder when next we will, like Cromwell's
Men, *eat biskett and cheese on Pentland's hills?*

Lothian burn

Up here, scarcely
Birdsong even: only

The labials and gutturals
Of this burn as it gurgles

Downhill, locality of accent
In vowel and consonant,

Each circumlocution
Through heather and sandstone

Traced by inflection
And sharp interjection

Until, in a mossy outcrop,
It comes to a glottal stop.

Westlandman

I lie here, *who for Christ's interest did appear*
Amongst those martyred on Rullion Green,
Having trudged from Dumfries through Ayr,
Knowing I was unlikely to see my family again;
Even then, not anticipating such slaughter
As would befall us, such numbers slain.
All to see the Episcopacy overthrown.

For days, drizzle steamed on a stew of limbs;
Those who fled being hewn down
In the mirk, between here and West Linton,
Their deathgasps reaching me like an exhalation.
So I lie, deep in Pentland bog, my person
Preserved perfectly, my spirit broken.
How many must perish in God's name?

Cherry Tree, in December

The cherry tree outside my study window, heavy
With blossom, is an elaborate bouquet,
A celebration or renewal of vows, this December day.

In your white dress, you walked smilingly
Down the aisle, then were whisked away
To the reception, the remainder of the lives we,

Together, would share. I regret only
That the years have passed so speedily;
Each moment, rushing by,

Leaving less time to enjoy.
I thank you for your love, and pray
Death when it comes, may come gently.

Meanwhile on this December day I see
From my study window, with a new intensity,
The delicate blossoms on that cherry tree.

Bedtime Story

'I don't like that one, Hansel
And Gretel, I told them so, little
Children enticed by a wicked witch
Into her marzipan cottage – such
Goings-on – too fearsome
For words, just before bedtime
Too: keep them up half the night.'

They recognise her plight,
Interpret it differently:
Grandma would be upset, you see
They confide later, from tact,
It's the old woman who gets cooked.

Interior

Our sitting-room at last furnished,
The clock ticks on its marble shelf,
Paintings hang more or less permanently,
A bronze horse makes space for itself

Behind the door. *Lares* and *penates* are placed
In the hearth. And notice
Our Lady of the Crinolines in the high chair,
Who we pretend does not exist.

Will she hold sway, I wonder,
In centuries' time? Or, this still a home,
Will it have become your ghost
That flits lovingly, from room to room?

Before Dark
(for Douglas Dunn)

They are so confident, the young, who strut
   Through the avenues that once were ours;
   So sure of themselves, knowing the future is theirs;
So cool and relaxed, as they scale the sweet
   Octaves of love; so self-possessed,
   Desire not yet on the wane, or become lust.

A bell sounds. The end of lectures for today.
   They fan out across the pastures
   Of the city, filling the nearest bars
Or returning to bed-sitters, wearily.
   The old smells linger: in Gibson Street,
   Curry powder; stale urine, from the Pewter Pot.

In my mind it will always be early winter
   In this Victorian sector of the city,
   Its terraces squandered by the University,
Heaped with swept leaves, a rotting umber;
   Kelvingrove a vast litter-bin; children
   Playing, generation upon generation.

I still have black-and-white snapshots taken
   In front of wrought-iron gates, in the early
   Days of the War; my father wearing a kipper tie.
How long I wonder, before our children,
   Asked who we were, explain idly if lovingly?
   In old age perhaps the rarest quality –

Certainly the one I most envy – is dignity,
   Especially in the face of pain. I cannot bear
   The thought of what loved-ones may suffer.
This is partly what drives me to poetry.
   The Missa Solemnis on, we sit and listen:
   From the heart, may it go to the heart again.

In the Gallery
(National Gallery, Edinburgh)

Heading for the National Gallery
To renew acquaintance with the Turner watercolours
I find I am formulating an analogy
Between this aesthetic pleasure and the urgency
With which we must face fierce

Mortality. For one month only of each year
Are these paintings on display,
Lest their colours
Succumb to the sun's rays.
So in marriage, we must seize

Every opportunity to act lovingly,
While fire is kept at bay. May
God in his mercy let us share
A little longer the charmed lives we bear.
So I make for these subtle blues and ochres,

Illustrations on smooth-grained paper
Of weightless lakes and rivers; trees
Like plumes, waterfalls suspended in mid-air;
On the bank, tiny transient figures –
Only when I get there to discover

This is already the first of February.
Accepting the fact as salutary, I take away
In my mind's eye a graver imagery;
Rembrandt, ageing; and Goya's seated doctor,
That basin of blood between his knees.

Turn of Century
(Tate Gallery)

Sickert's Minnie Cunningham stands alone
In the gloom at the Old Bedford,
From the top of her wide-brimmed hat
To the frilled hem of her gown
Rich red; one fore-arm
Languidly showing; face tilted
To catch the light's sheen.

She glows, glamour of loneliness.
Is it wistfulness merely,
Regarding an audience who are there
Or who have deserted her?
In her solitariness, a fragility
Which, garbed in white,
Would draw a-ghostliness about her.

What, almost a century ago,
Was to be her future?
Did she, like those back-cloth blooms
Left of frame, just fade away?
Is it their fragrance she inhales?
Explaining the slight pregnancy
Of posture, skittishness of pose?

To so much, there is no answer:
Like the Music Hall, gone
Into darkness; chandeliers brought down,
Stucco crushed to powder.
The death of a theatre, a whole era.
And she still solitary there –
Girlish in red, with so sombre an air.

Summer, Assynt
(for John Arnott)

Drumbeg

After three weeks' rain, Drumbeg is a swampland;
Suilven's tonsured skull lost
In mist. The forecasters extend
A blessing everywhere 'except the north-west'.

Marooned cattle peer
Through columns of moisture.
The lochs are less Landseer
Than Japanese watercolour.

By evening, we can see
The nearer hills. Under pale skies
Summer visitors emerge – like empty
Vessels, shifting in the breeze.

River Kircaig

Dear Lord Vestey
He had to write, *Please*
Accept my apologies
For fishing your water
With worm: otherwise
The ban would remain.
This after the discovery
Of two cock salmon
Along with his bait tin.

He gazes at anglers
In green chest-waders
Casting monotonously.
Suddenly his expression
Changes. Light glances
In his eyes as he sees,
Through the birch trees,
Two boys stealthily
Pursuing old ways...

Lochans

You, Loch Torr nan Hidhean
In the lee of Canisp, took some persuasion.
Loch a Braighe, you too showed a firm will
Before yielding a speckled fighter from your cross-ripple.

Despite your chill, Loch Gorm Mor,
A change of fly finally got your measure.
Then on the way home
To fail with you, lochan-of-no-name:

Naïve enough to try
And outreach pads of water-lily
I left in your dark bed an imprint deeper
Than I care to remember.

Departure

'Leave the cooker and kitchen
As you find them: clean.'
So on our last afternoon, as is proper,
We eliminate any reminder

Of our presence – so that whoever
Is next here
Finds no cup-ring or soup-stain,
But all spick and span.

As for the land around, little need
For circumspection. A neap tide
Laps where we clambered
Or sat pullovered –

While long before we drive away
We will trickle into anonymity;
The wader-prints round each lochan
Fished, by brimming waters filled in.

Offshore

Edging from shingle, the dinghy turns
  A tight half-circle, heading past the island
With its twisted pines, the twin horns
  Of rock guarding the bay, out across the sound.

Opposite the lighthouse we ship the oars
  And drift, lopsided. The boys let out handlines,
Each hook hidden in plastic and red feathers:
  Preferable, they feel, to bait moiling in tins.

Each, thinking he has a bite, finds weed.
  Small hands grow icier, with each haul;
Until only hope deferred, and pride,
  Sustain them. I wish them mackerel –

But find my thoughts turn, coldly, towards
  The foreign fleets who come
Trawling our shores; recalling the words
  Of those who say this was a fisherman's kingdom

Once, the surface phosphorescent from shoals
  Of herring feeding; holds crammed,
Decks silver with their scales.
  A bygone age, not likely to return; the unnamed,

As is customary, having destroyed. The boys,
  Eyes glistening with weariness and trepidation,
Wind in for the last time. Grown wise,
  They know I know there's nothing on the line.

End of Season, Drumelzier

Scarcely discernible, the line tautens
Against the current, then sweeps downstream.
The rod-tip shifts, dislodging a thin
Gleam of light. I spool in, cast again.

So the season ends. In near darkness
I try to reach the rise.
Something jumps. The circles
Are absorbed. Night closes in.

I stumble from the luminescent Tweed,
And trudge by torchlight to the farm,
Then home: waders discarded, I concentrate
On the winding road; watch hedgerows pass,

Sheer banks; branches like weed, overhead.
Sedgeflies smudge the screen. I bear left
Towards row upon row of lights that never meet.
In under an hour, I am crossing Princes Street.

So the close of each trout season
Brings its own desperation
To make up for lost days; a trek
To the river, a casting more frantic

Than judged. In life and love too, take care
To make the most of time – before,
Darkness encroaching, it is too late
For anything but the final onslaught.

Return Visit

Revisiting the Kibble Palace
after years of absence
is once more to witness
time's destructiveness.

The statues have lost
their piercing whiteness.
The herbage is less dense.
Even the glass dome seems

diminished in circumference.
To think my grandfather
carried me here; my sons in turn
scouring this pool for goldfish

and silted coins.
Now the lilies have gone.
And look how tawdry
the entrance has become.

When we leave, we cross
the shrunken Gardens,
not glancing behind us.
Later, at a distance,

I concede that what's lost
is within myself: the past
cannot be repossessed.
What future there is, is theirs.

Fieldfare

All that's left,
a ringed leg
on the shore
at Gullane,

that belonged
to a fieldfare
logged in Lincolnshire
four years

ago. At least
seven Atlantic
crossings since,
then caught

in mid-air
and spewed
from a gull's
gullet. In

the dawn light
you hug your pillow;
one finger wearing
its gold ring.

Recovery
(for Iain Crichton Smith)

1

You know now 'what inhuman pressures
keep a line of verse
on its own course'. The everlasting flowers
shiver in their vase.

And you in a strange place
believing your loved ones
have turned against you.
Behind incandescent mirrors

to be imprisoned...
All I can do is will you
patience and reassurance
and through them, peace of mind.

2

The poet's task, to seek
significant detail
in the face of horror.

It has always been so –
Yeats and Marvell writing
out of disturbance and war.

Like preserving a journal
through plague years.
And consider the chill

chambers, now ruined,
where were produced
these beautiful Books of Hours.

3

Or do you see yourself as Hamlet
in black, on black battlements waiting?
Do you hear the ghost clanking,
the jewelled clock within you, ticking?

Mercifully things are more mundane
on this side of the mirror – no one
plotting to kill you; no cup of poison,
no revenge tragedy, no treacherous queen.

If only the trees outside your window,
bristling with weaponry, could revert
to an uncomplicated green; the tides
off Oban sparkle, as they used to.

4

It must have been
like winter closing in,
the mind an icy
web: whereas

in your case, the metaphor
a sea-loch, its surface
seeming to freeze
yet retaining

the intellect's finery
and pulsing beneath,
those massive forces,
endurance and love.

Case Histories

Let us look first at Goldilocks
And these Three Bears. She takes,
For my money, the biscuit: a nosey
Missy, insensitive little hussy.

     Sir, if you're allocating responsibility,
     Mayn't we look at it this way:
     When he went out, Father Bear
     Could at least have bolted the front door.

You'll argue next if the small Bear had
Eaten his porrage, tidied his bed,
There'd have been no inducement for her to stay.
Then you'll tell me there's a history –

     – of deprivation in her family.
     Right. You refer too glibly
     (Evading the real issue) to 'her sort'.
     I'd like to ask for a background report.

Balderdash. You're so ready to berate
The law-abider, defend the deviate.
Anyway…let's turn to Snow-White who, as everyone knows,
Shacked up with those seven little fellows.

     They were her good news: if they'd been miffed
     Like the Bears, she'd have had short shrift.
     As it was she paid her way
     By doing the cooking and cleaning, daily.

Rubbish. She distorted the facts of life –
Said her stepmother went for her, with a knife.
In short, the classic schizophrenic.
With an attitude to apples, far from hygienic.

     I reckon, sir, what's bugging you
     Is: her story might be true.
     You Freudians are so unbending,
     You cannot stomach a happy ending.

Quixote Rides Again
(for Stephen MacDonald)

Throughout World War Two my great-uncle
Travelled the length and breadth of Ayrshire
Buying horses that looked on their last legs:
Seeing them carted off, folk would snigger
And place bets on how long each rickle
Of bones would survive. But to the dregs
Of stable and stall he'd administer
Poultices nightly, being known never to fail.

Before War ended the shire
Ran out of old nags, his main purchaser,
The Co-op, having Clydesdales enough. Then
We watched him go downhill rapidly,
Giving up the mart even, on Friday,
As though realising his course was run.
At last he was laid to rest in the land
He lived on. That day it rained and rained.

Other horses since have made their mark on me:
Funerary figures from the T'ang dynasty;
This or that city's rearing statuary;
The bronze mount in the Campidoglio;
That flayed beast, in Dostoyevsky;
Othello's neighing steeds; Faustus' *noctis equi*;
The hooves that go thundering through
Dante, entrapping life's energy.

Already leaves accumulate, as last year.
Limbs encased in glass, so brittle the air,
I hoist myself precariously over – and spur
My baleful Rozinante to a trot; soon to be headed
I know not where, frenziedly galloping
Through wastes of splintered mirrors...
Those grizzled visages...Cries go unheeded.
Dear Sancho, please...just one last thing.

The Return of Don Quixote

1 *The contest*

'I cannot wait, Sancho, for you or anyone.
   You must realise that, from our previous
   Existence. Resurrection now, however devious
A ploy, at least gives expression
To the demons within. You do not think, surely,
   That I could resist the temptation,
   On Dulcinea's behalf and my own,
To attack an age which behaves even less purely

Than ours? So, stand aside
   While I fasten the girths, and mount.
   There we are...my steed...Call me to account,
Sancho...whoa there...Indeed more, deride
My name and ancestry, whole right to knighthood,
   Should I come to grief. Stand back,
   While I ready myself for the attack.
Never adversaries so dastardly, by the rood.'

So saying, our jaunty hero caught
   His helmet on a branch whose backlash swept
   Him to the ground. Sancho could have wept.
But Quixote, coming to, had fought
The battle in his head, routed evil and returned
   For his fair maiden's hand. Compassion
   Was earned; and pity, after a fashion.
Sancho let him go, happy. His conscience burned.

2 *Quixote cogitates*

From my vantage point, olive trees extend
   Jagged branches, each silhouette
   Overlapping the next, cutting out light.
The sun fails to come through. The fiery brand
Of my beard has become a sheep's-wool hank
   Of nit and thorn, still my hallmark.
   What have I to protect me in the dark
But uncured leather; cuirass in gules, rank

As the carcass it was cut from; spear
  And shield of waning splendour;
  A bent blade whose shining hour
Appears fated to the life hereafter.
Envisaging myself I recall the adage
  No fool like an old one, but try
  With sporadic success to keep it at bay –
Believing age brings, with all else, self-knowledge:

As you assess me, so I see through you,
  Young caballeros eager to tilt at me,
  Eyes glinting with mockery,
Determined to put me down, your view
The fashionable one now. It is your will,
  Detectable in every glance,
  That I succumb to some fine lad's lance.
But think: I may be merely his windmill.

3 *Among the Ladies*

Quixote's horse's hooves go click-clack-click
  On the cobbles, like dominoes on a table
  (Or skulls, thinks Sancho, on friable
Board). 'She reeked of garlic,'
He cries vehemently – only to be rebuffed:
  'Master, her aroma was divine,
  I assure you.' 'Have you been at the wine?
What of the wart on –!' 'Her skin, soft

As a babe's.' 'If all you wanted
  Was to make a fool of me, deride my name,
  You could have had the grace to stay at home,
Not escort me here.' 'Master, you are enchanted,
That's what, by some malign spirit,
  To speak thus...' Further rejoinders
  Unuttered: 'When passion roars,
The eye can overlook demerit –

In other words, why study the mantelpiece
  When you're stoking the fire?'
  'You demean the most ancient order
Of chivalry.' 'Is not that the price

Of succumbing to Time's inexpressible passage,
   Don Quixote? Had you not detected
   How already we have been projected
Into a graver, much less courtly age?'

4 *Quixote goes fishing*

I lean over the boat's edge. This face
   Gleams back, through a web of waves:
   My own, but older; like leaves
Floating just beneath the surface.
I try casting on the other side:
   The features disintegrate.
   Nothing for it, but speculate
How soon my fate will be decided.

Meanwhile, is that abysmal creature
   Waiting for me, or going through hell
   On my behalf? Impossible to tell.
I open my mouth to shout: he does likewise, water
Pouring in. When I turn my visage away
   To avoid witnessing his pain,
   He for reasons best known
To himself does the same, simultaneously.

Head swimming, I cannot be sure
   Which of us is which; who is haunted
   By whom; whether he is my enchanted
Self, I the one struggling underwater.
Then it all comes back, too late:
   How I kissed my lips in the mirror
   When young; since when years of failure
(Row, Sancho, row...) have turned self-love to hate.

5 *Envoi*

'A bugle-call cracks black mirrors.
  Having for what seems centuries lain low
  In this hollow hill outside Toledo,
Our moment is come. With others
Of like metal, we must give our services
  To mankind, for freedom and the rights
  Of the downtrodden; with the Knights
Of the Round Table, step out to gain the prize,

Not for ourselves, but to dedicate
  To those ladies, Dulcinea and others
  Decorously loved, down the years.
So Sancho, to horse! The lanterns are lit;
Our ambling nags, steeds for a day,
  Ready; ourselves, bruises and agues forgotten,
  Eager for battle; weapons tempered to a fine
Point. Let us enter the fray...!'

'Don Quixote, when last we did this, Spain
  Was no longer the world we'd known
  But running with the blood of wounded men.
Must we risk our lives, again?'
'This time, dear Sancho, promises something rare:
  We shall attain to an incomparable purity –
  It is foretold – making us momentarily
Columns of whitest ash, in the receding air.'

At the Airport

We wave goodbye and watch them go,
Loved and familiar figures, through
The security check and on. In next to no
Time, they will descend on Ulster,
A charred land I lay no claim to
Other than through them, my parents-in-law.
They used to go by steamer from the Broomielaw;
Later, the shorter crossing from Stranraer

To Larne. Now the journey is more speedy,
But the gulf between us and the greenery·
Of Down and Antrim grown immeasurably –
So that what I see when people say
'Get the Army out' are two elderly
Heads on a pillow steeped with blood. To me
If not to most, politics are secondary
To the tug of personal loyalty.

On the periphery of their lives,
As they now are of ours,
We will be over the water
When our children are older,
Who already have privacies |
We cannot share... |
So much of life is a biting back of fear.
Their plane is ʳ speck in cerulean skies.

Change of Scenery

The train moves on, tunnel after tunnel,
My drowsing broken by intermittent hail
On thick glass. The horizon
Alternately dominates and retreats;
Plunging us from Tuscan sunlight,
Outcrop and turret clearcut,
Into a different season
Altogether: mediaeval cloud and rain.

Tempting, such is time's
Idealisation, to imagine
All we leave behind as permanently
Bathed in Botticelli
Blue; ourselves innocents hurled
Toward the crouching dark; victims
Of self-delusion, unwilling to recognise
Childhood is not the real world.

So with the Florentines –
Nostalgia for something lost
Overcome through delicacy
Of movement, fineness of line,
As in the *Allegory of Spring*
The Graces dancing in a ring
Against an orange-grove's liquidity
Are firm, under exquisite drapery.

The glass confronting us
Is both distancing device
And apt reminder
That we cannot penetrate
These mysteries, any more
Than our own. Sad simply
That unlike Art, Life
Seldom constructs Harmony from Strife.

Exploring those Quattrocentro woods
A traveller through time would see
Most visitations from the gods

As the squalid deflowerings they were;
And less likely encounter dryads at play
Than in darkness, from a wild boar
Maddened by pain, a huntsman's spear
In its side, go running for cover.

In Monte Mario
(for Patrick Rayner)

I lie staring at the ceiling, unable to sleep.
In the room opposite, surrounded by scalpels
And glass-topped bottles, Ettore restores lovingly
A Bassano landscape clamped to its easel.
Over my bed, in an oval frame, gilt but unadorned,
Is a sensuous Madonna ascribed to Leonardo:
The same model, as his Virgin
Of the Rocks; the tilt of her chin
Caught on canvas at the time of the Borgias;
Surveying this room, in a Rome torn by explosion;
Even in darkness, radiating tenderness.
Her presence makes me more tense than were any
Woman of flesh beside me. Each time I stretch
For the light-switch, a single mosquito
Settles just out of reach. At last I rise
And tiptoe murderously across the room –
To be drawn back to her portrait. So
Exquisite the dilemma: the wiry creature
Perches precisely on the nose of the Madonna.

'Springtime'

In front of me a girl with bare feet,
In a beribboned dress, picks white
Flowers in a field somewhere near Pompeii.

Each day I look at her, head straight,
Right hand outstretched as she delicately
Plucks the stem. Was she there that night

The lava flowed, birds shrivelled in the sky
And lovers turned to ash, where they lay?
If so, what had she done to deserve it?

I wonder, will it ever be
Springtime again, the blood flow freely;
Or has man blighted all hope of recovery?

We are on borrowed time, you and I,
And have been from the outset.
All that is left, is to live lovingly.

Stewart Conn was born in Glasgow in 1936, and brought up in Ayrshire. In 1958 he returned to live and work in Glasgow's Hillhead, close to the Botanic Gardens with their distinctive Kibble Palace. Married with two sons he now lives in Edinburgh, where he is a BBC radio drama producer.

He has published five books of poems. *Stoats in the Sunlight* and *Under the Ice* received Scottish Arts Council Awards, while *An Ear to the Ground* was a Poetry Book Society Choice.

His published plays include *The Burning, The King, The Aquarium, I Didn't Always Live Here, Thistlewood* and *Play Donkey*. His stage play *Herman* won an Edinburgh Festival Fringe First Award in 1981, and his dramatisation of *Blood Hunt* was recently shown in the BBC's Screen Two series.